A Brief Guide To God And The Soul

Edward Conklin Ph.D.

Edward Conklin

ISBN 978-0-9906457-5-7

Edward Conklin

Acknowledgments

During the course of life there came to visit for some time, a muse of inspiration to focus my attention on the origin of existence and how humans are a continuation of it. For this I am ever thankful. I also gratefully acknowledge and thank family, friends, and teachers for their love, support, and encouragement. I acknowledge and thank and am indebted to many who have come before and without whose efforts, findings, and recorded words, this work would not have been written.

Edward Conklin

Published works by Edward Conklin Ph.D.

Psychology of God and the Soul. (2016). Amazon Kindle and CreateSpace.

Meditations on God and the Soul. (2015). Amazon Kindle and CreateSpace.

A Brief Guide to God and the Soul. (2015). Amazon Kindle and CreateSpace.

In the Beginning: A New Theory of the First Religion. (2014). Amazon Kindle and CreateSpace.

Cosmos, God, and Soul. (2014). Amazon Kindle and CreateSpace.

From Tool-maker to God Maker. (2014). Amazon Kindle and CreateSpace.

Waves Rough and Smooth & the Deep Blue Sea. (2014). Amazon Kindle and CreateSpace.

Getting Back Into the Garden of Eden. (1998). University Press of America.

Edward Conklin

Introduction

This short work is a collection of brief essays, a distillation and amplification of previous published and longer works that deal with similar topics. The discussion that follows is a focus on metaphysical areas of inquiry such as the western concept of a human-like god and the human soul.

Is there a god? If the answer to the question is that there is a human-like god who made the environment and life, oversees and variously causes or controls events, and waits after death to reward or punish, this is a false and wrong answer. If the reply to the question is that a human-like god is an artistic model subjectively created by humans to explain where the environment and life came from, serves to imaginatively protect human life, and represents the potential of humans to know and do at a higher level, this is a true and right answer.

Since a religion cannot be classified as mathematics, and cannot be classified as a science, then religion should be more properly classified as art. The term "art" is defined as "works created by human skill and imagination." Just as are tool-making, invention, and the creative arts of theatre, film, literature, painting, and sculpture, the many gods and goddesses of religion, are also the result of artistic endeavor, the purely artistic subjective expression of creative talent. Religion must be studied for what it really is, a creative craft and imaginative artistic expression.

Historically very few individuals have correctly, yet indirectly and vaguely, alluded to the soul. I am the first to accurately identify, define, and discuss in detail what the soul actually is. The human soul as that which survives physical death has long been associated with reason, ethics, morals, and goodness yet in reality is none these. The soul of life consists of a relative and triune force of hunger for food, sex and reproduction, and aggression that enable living forms to survive life and also to continue to survive after physical death. These behaviors are the soul essence of life, in turn a continuation of the environment, and all is a dependent continuation of a nonhuman-like cosmological origin.

Edward Conklin

A Brief Guide To God And The Soul

Metaphysical

For each human there is a biological struggle of birth out of the womb and into an earthly reality to grow and physically mature. There are only a very few individuals that exert the effort to have a later second birth into the spirit or "attitude of knowledge," and make the effort to comprehend the deeper ground of existence and essence of life. These few humans can turn away from the distractions of everyday life to see and successfully comprehend. What follows is for the few who seek the second birth of knowledge.

For the vast majority of humans, life is a quest to survive a daily existence of illness, accidents, aggression, and other humans. Everyday reality, as a quest for physical and emotional survival, is true for the majority of the population or 99.9999999 percent. For the other .000000001 percent there is a metaphysical quest to comprehend where the environment and life comes from, what is the animating essence of life, and what happens when life arrives at its destination of death.

Humans have a strong metaphysical interest in where life has come from, how things happen, and what happens after death. The area of philosophy known by the Greek word metaphysics, literally means, the study of what is "beyond the physical." The traditional focus has been to investigate from what and where the environment and life has come from and what moves all things into, through and out of existence. Wisdom seeks to discern what is behind the phenomena of the environment and life. What is the unseen force that moves nature (Latin natus, to be born) and the seeming unlimited universe and the limited function of living cells? The movement of life is a continuation of the environment and the forces and energies of the universe. It is a worthwhile endeavor to acquire knowledge of the metaphysical basis of existence, to discern and comprehend the movement of the environment, life, and humans. Simply stated as a philosophical axiom, the impetus for and the relative motion of the environment and life, are a continuation of a cosmological force.

Modern physicists have searched for and found the "meta" or beyond of energy and forces, and have also found the cosmological forces of "dark matter" and "dark energy" that move together and move apart the massive galaxies of the universe. Cosmological force is located everywhere, is unlimited and omnipresent and so is not in any particular limited place. It is not a phenomenon, it does not appear as an object of perception, and its presence can only be intuited from observation of the relative movement of the environment and living forms. The study of life known as biology has produced the reliable knowledge that life comes from and is dependent upon the earth environment. But what moves life? The sciences of biology and psychology have stopped short and have not considered the metaphysical vastness to which the environment and life are but a miniscule part. Life from bacteria to plants, animals, and humans, are a continuation of change of the environment that moves as a continuation of a cosmological force.

Life is a relative changing mirage, a series of moments, tasks, struggles and conflicts appearing and vanishing in endless space and time. On either side of each now moment there exists a cosmic vastness, masked with relative individual thoughts, interests, relationships, and goals. Relative time of changing reality events obscure what is an unchanging timeless dimension of reality. A cosmological force ever exists and yet appears only as nothing or space, and from it exists all that is tied to as time and change.

Amid an environmental sea of changing sensations, the human brain/mind by necessity seeks stability. Lacking objective stability, the essential subjective criteria is to locate that which is prior to the sequence of all relative change. A necessary criteria for many is that the first origin of existence and human life must especially be human-like. Humans are limited in strength and time, and yet they vaguely recognize the origin of their condition to come from what is unlimited and timeless. For many the origin of life cannot possibly be an unhuman-like cosmological force but for the necessity of limited knowledge, must be a very human-like god.

Humans exist in a stable but uncaring environment, among mostly uncaring other living forms, and aside from family and friends, among other uncaring fellow humans. Since the predominant reality is uncaring, humans conceive the idea of a caring human-like god and laden it with words to subjectively comfort themselves. Yet a human-like god is subjective and so cannot ever objectively care for humans. A human-like god is a mediate model, a parent figure and shared silent witness to the good and bad interactions of each human. This conceived and believed mechanism of a parent figure functions to mediate social behaviors. An innate evolved human ability for empathy (feeling with) and conscience (knowing with) is paired with an imagined bigger than life parent figure and over-seer.

The conscience that is innate in humans as that which judges and imposes guilt, has been glorified and projected outside of an individual. The intelligent see through the popular delusion of a human-like god. They utilize it for their own ends, such as to instill parental social order and to inspire the necessity of individuals to daily shoulder burdens and to toil at work and in wars. A human like god is an ego, an "out-go" of what is inside in the direction outside toward what is strong and good, to go in the direction of where life came from, to go in the direction of what made life and what might care for it. A universal human-like god is only a self-important crown that humans have placed upon their own heads. A human-like god has been "invented," conceived inside and vented outside as real. It is helpful to have a human-like model to identify where life comes from as only a human-like beginning is plausible for the naïve. For a theist, the environment and life, and the energies of elements and forces are not seen as an ongoing process of evolution.

In the Garden of Eden story humans are banished by an angry human-like god. Disobedience is the cause of the sin (Hebrew hata, separation) or separation from a supernatural first father, portrayed as the cause of a sequence of biological fathers. In a long sequence of evolving biological fathers, to conceive and insert a first father in a sequence of natural fathers is ludicrous. Fossil evidence supports the view that supported by the environment, all of life evolved from single cells, and evolved to multicellular, reptile, mammal, and hominid ancestors.

Without a human-like god the environment is uncaring. Only life cares for life, cares to consume other life forms, cares to have sex and reproduce, cares to be aggressive in obtaining food, and cares to aggressively defend individual life. A human-like god is a comforting way of identifying a human origin and is also a way of accepting a greater reality of immense uncaring dimensions of space and time. The concept of a human-like god is a utilitarian tool of assurance, assistance, and authority, during the agonizing times of existence. A human-like god is a subjective human insistence for assistance to subsist.

Pondering the origin of existence, theistic religious artists, incorrectly known as founders, conceived of a human-like god, spoke about it, and assistant artists wrote down their exploits. Taking the theistic art of a human-like god for reality, is in lieu of any real knowledge of how all things are a continuation of a nonhuman-like and nonlocal (a physics term for the religious word omnipresent) cosmological force. All theistic scriptures ever written are but a conceptual ménage of empty words, a human artistic verbal portrait that sketches a human-like god in an attempt to reduce pessimism and to promote optimism. The scriptures convey a false confidence that life is a carefully thought out plan by a god. In reality there is only a frail human "lay track as you go" of a human freight train ride on the rails of a daily unknown journey.

The message of theism that the origin of existence is human-like, is inculcated over time and accepted as real. In reality the message is merely an immature and obtuse conceived explanation, a hypostatization and projection. The origin of existence is not something human-like that "knows" but is something unhuman-like that "goes and grows." All that moves is in relative motion to the origin of existence. Life must be perceived for what it is; a continuation of a changing environment that exists only as a continuum of a dynamic cosmological force. There is no disconnection or separation from a cosmological force. There is only an ongoing failure of perceptual clarity caused by the clouded insertion of a human-like god, in the unerring natural cause and effect sequence of the environment and life.

A cosmological force that comes from nothing else is beginningless and endless, and exists as a surround outside and permeates inside living forms. A single cosmic force brings forth a range of relative forces, energy, and forms. The environment is continually in motion, and living cells and organs of life are always moving and functioning. Sensations of the senses are continually changing, as are brain/mental processes of memory, images of future time, and conceptions. Inquisitive individuals continue to struggle to comprehend the cosmos, the behavior of the environment and living forms, and individual physical and mental behaviors.

Order and Disorder

The environment consists of both order and disorder. Life as a continuation of the earth mimics this dynamic. What moves inside a living cell is a continuation of the changing moving environment, and both are a continuation of a greater cosmological force. The origin of both order and disorder is not a human-like caring god but an uncaring cosmological force. This is why both order and disorder equally reign in the universe. Life is an orderly progression of growth yet is prone to the disorders of genetic cellular and organ dysfunctions, and injury. Humans all too often find it difficult to control the outside environment and to maintain personal relationships. They also find it just as difficult to order what is inside so as to maintain physical and mental health. The vast majority of individuals are not up to the task of observing, learning, or reducing disorder and living a life of order. It is difficult to maintain order of the human body, prone as it is to accidents, disease, and human aggression. It is also difficult to maintain order of the brain/mind processes, prone to confusion, emotional conflict, worry, ignorance, superstition, and pathology.

It is in the fertile ground of the brain/mind response to disorder of the environment, disorder with others, and disorder inside the body and brain that the idea of a human-like god grows. There are many psychological disorders and physical diseases. If enough inside and outside disorder is experienced, then a human-like god is imagined by humans to impose at least a semi-order. The god of western religion is a symbol of omnipotent order and is reputed to reward an orderly life on earth with the afterlife order of a heaven. The human-like god is also said to punish the disorder of life with the disorder of an afterlife, namely hell.

Praise of a human-like god by humans is in reality only narcissistic lauding of abstract concepts and words as to their own origin. The act of praising a god is also recognition of human potential to know and interact at a higher level. Experiencing a lack of control and insecurity in life, humans place a human-like god around and above themselves. Having a lack of control with ageing and dying humans also conflate a human-like god with an afterlife dimension. The traditional task of the human-like god is to save the soul of an individual. It is obvious that the god never bothers to perform this task for humans while living. After a life on earth, a further task of the god is to separate the good from those who are evil, and to reward or to punish.

A human-like god is also a symbol, a sign that points the way to a higher level. The word "symbol" is defined as, "something that represents or stands for something else." The word is derived from the Greek language (syn, together and bole, a throwing, and ballein, to throw). The word "god" is a symbol, a throwing together and conflating the origin of the environment and life with human attributes that conceives the origin of existence to be a human-like.

The word god is an analogy, the comparing of "this with that," of humans with the origin of the environment and life on earth. A god is an analogical way of saying what the cause of reality events is, and that it is human-like. Agreeing there is a god is quite similar to a bouncing ball that is utilized to follow song lyrics projected onto a screen so all those assembled can sing along in harmony. The idea of a human-like god projected in imagination persuades those participating in the singsong view that the god is not only subjective but also objective. A greater human-like god contributes to peace and harmony among humans. Otherwise, without a greater will to enforce and mediate between the environment and among other willful humans, fear, conflict and aggression would be much more prevalent.

There is infinite order and disorder but not an infinite intelligence. It is quite evident on earth that intelligence evolves and is finite. Order and disorder consist of causal change not the whim of a human-like god. There is a cosmological cause of all relative cause and effect change, as one phenomenon changes and effects another. There is no intelligence beyond the order and disorder of the whole environment and life. In modern times it is easy to observe the fossil evidence that life evolved from viruses and single cell life forms into multicellular life. Intelligence is an ability that only slowly evolved with humans. It is the lesser human intelligence of prejudice and ignorance posits a greater first intelligence of a human-like god.

Humans need a greater intelligence of a god to rely on rather than an unknowing cosmological force. In limited human thinking, there must be an intelligence that has enough knowledge to create or make the environment and living forms. This intelligence that makes an order also makes a lot of disorder, makes good and a lot of evil, in the environment and in the human body. While much in individual life is wanted, such as money, possessions, health, happiness, and a spouse, just to name a few, much more of life experience is unwanted; such as, accidents, divorce, sadness, poverty, physical and mental illness, interpersonal conflict, crime, war, ageing, and death.

A human-like god has been generated by humans for humans, a powerful personality to control an uncontrolled and semi-orderly cause and effect cosmos of unceasing change. A human-like god is a way of turning away from the earth to the origin of the environment and life. To not turn to something or to an impersonal cosmological force is not a viable option. A human-like god who commands is but the wishful imagination of humans. A commander of the environment and life and also what is after death, even though imaginary, brings comfort to many who can command very little in life.

Unknowing

Not knowing where they came from except by wandering from somewhere over the horizon, early humans conceived that their life just like animal and plant life, came from the body of the earth, just as they came from the body of their mother. Eventually humans began to ponder about where the earth came from, and if the earth is the first mother who gave birth to them, then where is the first father? Their attention was of course drawn away from the earthly mother to look at the vast sky activity, the moving sun, moon, stars, planets, comets, and asteroids. Early humans then began think of the unseen cause of this cosmic motion in terms of strength and power, and saw the activity as that of an unseen male gender. Early humans looked away from the earth and began to think in terms of a first father of the sky.

For Paleolithic humans, the earth was thought to be the mother that gave birth to life from within the soil, dens, and caves of the earth. Judging from the artifacts of stone, bone, engraved female Venus figures, and cave paintings in France and Spain, humans conceived of and thought they came from the interior of the earth. Eventually the moving forms of the sky environment were given human-like attributes to be gods such as the planets Venus, Mars, and Jupiter. Time and place of the environmental forms became important, as the sun, moon, planets, eclipses, and constellations appeared on the horizon. Observation of the movement of massive environmental forms to a certain place and time for early humans was evidence of intentions of greater human-like gods.

Perplexed and alone in the endless cycles of time, so as not to feel lonely on the earth with its myriad dangers, humans began to think of the first father of humans as having strength to protect them and if long lasting or eternal, humans would never be alone. The earth mother was solid and real while humans could only conceive of the vast sky activity to be the active strength and power of an unseen first father. The earth was a local anthropomorphism, while the unseen yet active in the sky first father was an abstract anthropomorphism. This is the basis of theism and the necessity of faith; trust that what moves all things into existence is an unseen human-like male god. The root of all theistic religions is the male ego, the much larger male maker of the environment and life, rather than attribute the origin of life to the large, but comparatively smaller, female earth.

Need For A God

The important announcement theists make, that there is a human-like god, is to say the beginning of existence is known, and that humans have a higher unachieved potential. While bringing comfort, the first meaning is false while the second meaning is true but difficult to develop. Hence the need for a god to help those who need assistance at some time or other. A human-like god is a way humans elevate themselves to a higher level, a conceived way of reaching for and keeping company with higher ethical qualities.

Christian theologians are proud in their having special knowledge of a "theos," a human-like god. The stories of how the god created the universe and gave commandment laws, are presented in various languages of Hebrew, Greek, Latin, and English. Unfortunately theologians lack the ability to comprehend how a human-like god was psychologically developed in the Middle East and later adopted as a needed utilitarian tool of European thought to assist rulers in governing the populations of various countries.

It is a liberal modern view that a good human-like god exists and that existence and humans are good. For as the Greek sage Bias of Priene (circa 500's BCE) briefly and truthfully said, "Most men are bad." The Greek philosopher Heraclitus (circa 500's BCE) also said, "The bad are many, the good are few." Much truth in a few words that refer to the will-to-live essence of individual existence; the hunger for food, sex and reproduction, and aggression. This is the greater predominance in human behaviors, not the later evolved ability to measure or reason.

Existence and humans are not good or at most only half good which is why humans needed and developed a greater human-like god in the Middle East, Europe, and western countries in general. Existence is beset with a predominance of struggle and conflict; many humans lack goodness. Humans have attempted to make existence good with a god and with group will of a government. In the last few hundred years the development of science and technology has accelerated in an effort to make existence more tolerable if not good. Yet humans continue to struggle and to be in conflict with the environment, other life forms, and each other.

A humanlike god is subjective not objective. The ego of a human-like god is only a human generated word symbol conceived to bolster and to protect the human ego. Western religion worships the ego of a human-like god as it represents the higher potential of the human ego rather than the lower potential that is most common in society. The common representation for lower human potential is a devil or demon.

If a human-like god will not save humans, then for Christians it is hoped the god's god-human son will save them. If Jesus is accepted to be a real person who lived in the Middle East, to say he is the son of a god is also an attempt to make the subjective view of a god to be more real, acceptable, and believable. For Christians circa 100 CE, it was time for a loving god as the classical gods rarely made life better for the average person. The Jewish god rewarded little and punished quite severely at times with curses, floods, and plagues. The uneducated and poor during the time of Jesus, accepted the view of a loving father-like god. The view continues with the uneducated and poor and general population in modern times and illustrates the dire human need for affection and love that is difficult to find from other humans.

When an average individual comes to experience the transience and terrors of existence he turns to religion (Latin re, again and relegere, to connect) to find protection. During troubling times most individuals usually do not turn to a cause and effect process but to a human-like god, of the Middle East variety, the first father who began the continual change of life as hunger for food, sex and reproduction, and aggression. The conceived notion of a human-like god is a common and popular view that is elevated by humans to an exalted status of theological knowledge when in reality the alleged objective knowledge is but a lower level of subjective artistic imagination. A human-like god is only an imaginary and artistic representation of humans. A higher human-like presence above the earth represents a role model for human potential; to achieve a higher level of comprehension and ethics.

The general population, and especially the uneducated and poor, find it difficult to endure life without the imagined and believed support of a human-like god. Human reliance on only individual endurance in life soon wanes, and the relief of physical death can become less feared and even more appealing. Saying there is the ego of a human-like god who endures and ever exists, so then can the ego of an individual human endure life and ever exist beyond physical death. To have a greater knowing and intelligent human-like god is an effort to be optimistic and to not have a god is to be pessimistic about a non-human reality of cause and effect forces and energies.

Motto

The motto "In God We Trust" imprinted on American currency is vague. The word "god" is a generic term for any male deity. The English word god is derived from the German word "gott" and was taken originally from the Viking male deity "Wodan or Godin." Most all gods have names such as Zeus, Mars, Shiva, El, Abba, and Allah, just to name a few.

So what is the name of the god that the United States refers to on its money? Is the god unknown? If so, the citizens of the United States are trusting in an unknown god. Is this wise to do? Or perhaps the name of the god is known but is intentionally not revealed and kept secret. Since the motto is printed on coins and paper money, does it refer to a god of money or wealth? Perhaps the generic term of god is but a religious symbol and an equivalent for the original secular motto of "E pluribus unum," Latin meaning, "Out of many one." In any case, the god's name and identity should be announced, and if this cannot be done then the god referred to must be deemed vague and the motto should forthwith be removed from all United States currency.

Topsy-Turvy

For many evolving years, various areas of human comprehension have been and continue to be topsy-turvy or upside down. Many a person on earth say it is true that there is a male human-like god. Along with this they think there exists a special presence inside the human body that survives physical death. The human-like god is said to be good yet an excess of evil reigns upon the earth. The human soul is said to be good yet is also afflicted with the evils of existence.

Middle Eastern and Western populations who accept these topsy-turvy views, suffer from two mass delusions or mistaken ideas. The first delusion is that a monotheistic human-like god exists objectively and is true and real. Realistically, any and every human-like god is a fabrication of the human brain/mind. In reality there is only a subjective human-like "god" and a real objective cosmological "ground" from which all things come and are a dependent continuation. There is no god, however, there is a ground of cosmological force from which the environment dependently goes as changing motion and from which life on earth dependently grows.

If humans in the past and theists today do not know much about the environment and life, then surely some greater intelligence does. For human imagination, going back in time there would have had to be a very first parent of humans, not so much a physically weak parent having a birth canal but a strong male parent. For the average person, what moves and forms the environment and life has to be a generic human-like god. A human-like god is the myopic metaphysics of the general population, and the uneducated and poor. A human-like god serves as companionship when other humans are not helpful and the environment is unsafe.

The scientific name for the human species is the Latin term Homo sapiens sapiens or "man wise wise." It is obvious that this name is a misnomer and the more correct appellation for the species is "homo vulnerabilis inops" or "man vulnerable helpless." An individual is conceived in the throes of passion or lust and if development goes well is born vulnerable and helpless. Humans live vulnerable lives and are helpless when an accident, disease, or violence happens, and vulnerable and helpless when ageing and death occurs. Each is vulnerable and will soon come to experience helplessness and some unavoidable pain and agony. To remedy being vulnerable and encountering fearful and helpless situations, imaginary knowledge of a human-like god is conceived. The notion of a human-like god is the human effort to help themselves. Humans deal with their much less than perfect intelligence and flawed biology by conceiving of a most perfect human-like god and forefather. A god is a vicarious way to control for humans who are helpless and a place of worship is a place of rest and safety from harmful daily life. A human-like god is a product of knowledge, a comforting conception, as a way of identifying where humans can obtain strength when life becomes vulnerable and helpless. To compensate for vulnerability and helplessness, a human-like god is born in the human brain.

Dying and death necessitates a greater human-like presence to take care of vulnerable and helpless humans, otherwise a godless afterlife would be frightening. The human-like god is only myopically interested in the dying and death of humans as there is not any literature of a theistic god favoring animals or vegetation during life or after death. The reality of a dimension that is natural or unhuman-like is not comforting, and mere cause and effect of life and death cannot care for humans. Most humans take care of themselves and others poorly while living on earth, therefore any deceased soul or spirit could not possibly be of assistance to another in the afterlife. Only an imagined greater human-like god would be helpful.

First Father Argument

In the beginning, the omnipotent human-like god of Genesis created all things with thoughts and words. The human-like god dogmatically presented in the Old and New Testaments and the Quran, and other theist texts, is what I refer to as the "first father argument." In the study of philosophy, a philosophical argument is not a verbal or physical fight but is defined as "an attempt to persuade another to a point of view or course of action." In other words, the person presenting the argument wants to convince others to see or do something in a certain way. The argument is specious as lacking a knowledge of the evolution of species, of necessity there had to be a first father of all later fathers and mothers.

Theists including Jews, Christians, Muslims and others, depend on an inner conceived and outer located human-like god. Theists lack comprehension and knowledge of both biology and psychology inside, and the outside environment. The brain/mind of a theist imagines a primal timeless first father as the origin of the time sequence of all father and mothers. A human-like god is a conceived "word compass" pointing in the direction of the beginning and especially the first parent. Yet the intentional compass points in the wrong direction. The true location of a human-like god exists only as a conceived view inside of the human brain/mind and not ever outside.

A god is the inner conceived and outer directed way to resolve inevitable problems of living. The way to the highest is conceived inside the brain/mind, and attention in milliseconds is shifted outside to a human-like god. A god is only a conceived symbol for the higher knowledge of the brain when it is not overwhelmed by the lower behaviors of the body needs of hunger, sex and reproduction, and aggression. When a person converts to accept the view of a human-like god as real, they are in reality accepting a role model for their own higher potential, especially as a way of succeeding in life and getting along with others known as ethics.

A human-like god is like a carrot placed before a donkey to get it to carry or pull a load from one place to another. Similarly both the crafty and sincere, place the concept of a human-like god before the gullible general population, especially the uneducated and poor, and before those who sincerely strive to live a good and ethical life. The carrot of a human-like god is placed above individuals to lighten the burden of life, and also dangled before an individual to ensure choices that lead to a heaven rather than a hell. At the end of a day's toil the donkey may finally obtain the carrot as a satisfying reward, just as the concept of a human-like god is introjected or swallowed daily to provide rewarding individual satisfaction.

If told to when young, the concept of a human-like god hovers in the subconscious background so that conscious attention and memory can consult and appeal to the concept during occasions of struggle, trauma, failure, or to thank for individual success in life. Certainly many hold to a helping human-like god through the struggle of life and death. Yet it is ironic and some might say moronic, to cling to what is credited with bringing humans into the struggle, stress, and pain of life and death.

The great "sin" of life is the behavior of living; the hunger for food that leads to the death of other living forms, sex and reproduction that leads to ageing and death of the individual and eventually the offspring, and aggression that leads to conflict, injury, and death. Sin (Hebrew hata, separation) is separation from a human-like origin that does not engage in these behaviors. However, in the books of record in the Old Testament the god also cursed, destroyed humans and life in a flood, and inflicted aggression (Deuteronomy 32:39-42). The god also received burnt offerings that were "a sweet savour unto the Lord." (Leviticus 1:9) Finally in the New Testament the god exhibited a need to have offspring and so impregnated a young virgin following her first menstruation of puberty as was customary of the time. So evidentially the higher first father god succumbs to aggression, hunger, and reproduction, and so exhibits what is seen to be lower human traits.

A first father as a human-like god is a human way to relate human behaviors to a model origin. This is where ethics begins, positing the notion there exists what does not display the behaviors of hunger, sex, and aggression, yet is the greater origin of these behaviors in humans. These biological behaviors had a beginning and sequence of evolution that was not observable to humans of the time, therefore a human-like god was conceived to explain them.

A first father as a greater creator was early conceived and since then has been inflated into a school of theology that continues to persuade and guilt many simple-minded followers to accept the simple artifice. When the average person thinks of a human-like god, it is usually in situations of personal need, conscience, or death, and then occurs an appeal to a first father of human-kind. This mental maneuver continues to be so accepted and unexamined that it is deemed normal and mandatory. However, a first father is an artificial terminus in an extended line of evolution traced with evidence to earlier and simpler life forms and a supportive environment and beyond to palpable energies and forces. The first father is only an immature and juvenile species way of identifying a beginning and a refuge of care. In reality a first father is an artificial beginning, and the evidence for an uncaring long sequence of evolution of the environment and life has only recently been observed in unearthed fossil and artifact evidence.

When humans heap praise on a human-like god, they denigrate and obscure the process of cause and effect change, of what is divine (Latin di, into, and the verb vine, meaning to grow). What is divine is not the noun of a human-like god but the verb of the dividing and growing immanence and continuation of a cosmological force. The ignorance and emotion of conceiving and utilizing a theological genealogy of a first father who created the first humans, conceals the true cosmological heritage and genealogy of evolution.

Christians advocate the view that a Middle Eastern fatherly god had a "begotten" son with an adolescent girl as mother. Realistically, no part of the human reproductive anatomy or virgin vagina has ever given birth to a god. The only part of the human anatomy that has ever conceived and given birth to a god or a god's son is the human brain. Realizing that theistic religions consist only of metaphorical folktales, evokes a new improved and more truthful Lord's Prayer:

O' Cosmological Force, omnipresent and omnipotent, yet unknowing and nameless;
From it the motion of the environment and the willing movement of life is a continuation,
As a continuation of it, comes all that exists on earth and other vast dimensions of space and time.
As a continuation of it, living forms grow day by day to destroy and consume each other for food;
As a continuation of it, humans struggle through life for money, incur debt, and find little or no forgiveness from debtors.
From it, comes both the good and the evils of existence evermore.
So Be It.

Soul

Many humans hope that some kind of non-physical energy which moves the body, will separate from and will survive the ageing and death of physical cells and organs. Therefore, the second topsy-turvy human delusion is that the human soul is wonderful and good and deserves to be, and must be saved from existence and from non-existence. This theistic way of thinking is the appealing fraud of a saving god of the Middle East, the westernized savior religion of Christianity.

The human brain/mind correctly intuits there is a soul but in error conceives of it as good and as related to a good human-like god. Of all body parts the cerebral brain considers its own functions to be higher and conceptualizes and imagines a higher origin as a human-like intelligent god. In the estimation of the cerebral brain, the organs of the body are essential but lower functioning, yet it is also said by theistic religion to contain a special animating presence made by a human-like god. A human-like god is a model of good and the human soul is said to be good and worth saving, yet the soul of life also wills evil toward others.

Popular theism is a psychological reaction formation in response to the risks, dangers and fatalities of living. In contrast, the nonhuman-like Brahman in Hinduism, the nonhuman-like Chinese Tao, and nontheistic Buddhism are true perceptual religions. Nontheistic religions also have the insightful view that humans are immortal as they are connected to some greater cosmological force of which individual willing is a continuation. All living things grow from within outward. The maker of the body exists inside as a continuation of an outside environment and cosmological force. The forming and growing behavior of life is a continuation of the behavior of the environment that is in turn a continuation of the behavior of a cosmological force. The behavior of the environment and behavior of life is not at all related to the storied behavior of a human-like god.

As a continuation of a cosmological force, a soul is a ductile local force with nonlocal (quantum entangled parts interacting at a distance) properties that move and shape differing living forms. It exists in the smallest and largest of living things as a supportive movement and vague intention of stimulus-response "doing and knowing" to find nourishment, to have sex and/or to reproduce, and be aggressive. Subconscious soul sensing has evolved from single cell life to conscious knowing processes of the human brain/mind dynamic. Human secondary conscious rational thinking is stimulated to act by a primary subconscious irrational soul force of hunger, sex, and aggression.

The soul has long been associated with reason and ethics but in reality is neither of these. The soul of life consists of the relative and triune force of hunger for food, sex and reproduction, and aggression; the main human realities. Therefore, food stores and restaurants are ubiquitous in towns, cities, and along most inhabited roadsides. Sex and reproduction are not as frequent as daily food consumption, yet human population continues to increase. As both individuals and populations increase in size, the quality of life for both is degraded. When the quality of life degrades, aggression ensues as interpersonal conflict, crime, and war. While humans do cooperate, there is a predominance of aggression. Directed aggression to get the better of each other verbally and physically results in threats, intimidation, lying, deception, jealously, envy, competition, struggle, pernicious gossip, avoidance, confrontation, plotting, lawsuits, injury, crime, and violent conflict of war. This is everyday human reality and for the average person only the fervent held view of a good human-like god can control and moderate these many insidious and brutish behaviors.

What many are unable to perceive and articulate is the reality of the human soul that consists of a triune force of hunger, sex and reproduction, and aggression. These subconscious forces easily overpower conscious attention and direct reasoning ability. The triune soul force makes it difficult to trust the human ability to reason, so theists stubbornly and stupidly insist on a higher authority as an imaginary human-like god mediator between humans and the environment and between human and human.

The human soul is a triune force that is difficult to control with human reason. Ethical behavior is traditionally imposed on humankind through general agreement that a human-like god exists and that the god takes an interest in human behavior. In reality, ethics should not be based on a human-like god but on exploration of what is inside and outside. Exploration of body and brain/mind functions brings about ethics by seeing a shared continuation of conditions of the environment that in turn is a continuation of a cosmological force. In so doing this sane way of seeing leads to discarding the long-held less than sane yet utilitarian view of a human-like god. The false notion of a human-like god is a conceived and comforting support to many rather than face the true reality of where the environment and soul of life comes from, an unhelpful and unmoral bleak ground of a cosmological force.

Triune Soul

The soul of life is a cosmologically instilled force. The soul has not come from a human-like god that breathed air into a shaped human form, or a result of supernatural surgery of the ribs as artistically portrayed with words in the biblical Genesis tale. The story is a marred metaphor, a crude unknowing that tells the tale of when a human-like god made animals and humans, there was no hunger, no sexual knowledge and reproduction, and no aggression of animal or human. Yet as the metaphorical story unfolds, the triune soul force of life is portrayed to be a curse from a god. The curse was to till the soil of the earth to appease human hunger, knowledge of human sexuality was obtained by disobediently taking it from a special Tree of Knowledge of Good and Evil, and aggression is portrayed as having a root in envy and jealousy of one brother toward another.

This triad is reflected in the behavior of the human-like god of the Tanak or Old Testament. The god began existence with the aggression of cursing humans, (Genesis 3:14-19) and later destroyed most of them in a horrific flood (Genesis chapters 6, 7, 8). The god also received burnt food offerings through the sacrifice of animals. Later in the New Testament the same god reproduced himself sexually with a pubescent girl (Matthew 1:18-25, Luke 1:26-38). Such is the amusing exploits of the Jewish god.

The curse of life by the human-like god in the metaphorical Genesis tale is in reality the innate evolving triune soul force. In reality, humans are cursed and condemned but not by a human-like god. The curse of life that humans are condemned to is that they must obtain food, must have sex that often leads to reproduction and toil to care for the young, and have to act with mild to bestial aggression. Such is the curse of the cause and effect sequence. Fraught with changing conditions inside the body and outside, and unexpected consequences experienced as chance, these essential behaviors of life in time become either addictive, depressing, futile, meaningless, or destructive.

Life whether waking or sleeping, is seldom comfortable for long. Life hungers for food every few hours, seeks sex and orgasm and to reproduce and care for and worry about the young, and seeks to be competitive and aggressive. Each individual has to continually adjust to the curse on an hourly and daily basis. What is satisfying for a time soon becomes dissatisfying, then boring, and subsequently aggression is directed to another person, thing, or situation. Relief occurs by moving on to another temporary satisfaction, and life goes on.

One third of life is spent in nighttime sleep while the other two thirds is the semi-sleep of daily living. Human life passes quickly and in the end grows old and feeble, and then each independent individual has to submit to and be dependent on those around them. Family members while supportive, are also distractions to a focus of attention, perception, and comprehension of life. Acts of eating food, having sex and children, and aggression, are the triune soul essence of life, in turn a continuation of the environment, and all is dependent on a cosmological force.

As a continuation of a cosmological force, the essence of the environment and life is both an outer and inner motion of change. The essence of the triune soul is popularly considered to be a non-divine and non-godly dynamic of existence. The human predicament and dilemma is that in reality, an individual is "dammed" not in relation to a human-like god who can control or stop humans from a particular activity but by the separating limitation of not seeing that a triune soul force is a continuation of a cosmological force. Christian theology refers to a triune god of Father, Son, and Holy Spirit. This is a mythic distortion of a triune soul projected outside that in reality is located inside that is a continuation of the environment, and a cosmological force that moves all. The greater animating Spirit anthropomorphized as a human-like god and first father outside is a cosmological force, while a "spirit" inside is an evolved human ability to reason and think, and the "soul" is a triune force of hunger for food, sex and reproduction, and aggression.

Superior Soul.

In the biblical Genesis story, a superior human-like god and first father created inferior humans. Later in the New Testament the same god decided to procreate with an inferior human. To do so he chose a pubescent girl and "begot" according to Catholic doctrine, a fully god and fully human son. The son called Jesus is deemed superior to the first made two humans, and all later sexually reproduced humans. Christian theologians portray Jesus as exceptional since he came from the body of a god. The god's superior son also serves to inspire all other "inferior" humans. In reality the portrayed inferiority of the human condition is a judgment by vulnerable and often helpless humans plagued by the outside environment, other life forms, and inside by the triune soul force of life.

The much vaunted faith in a human-like god is only a deluded trust in human imagination. The potential to be superior as an evolved ability to think at a higher level, is projected outside to reside as an abstract and distant human-like god. Humans imaginatively and artistically project and portray their own higher potential. A superior first father is also an artistically devised portrait using human attributes to explain where the environment and life came from. Life comes from the body of the environment and from a nonlocal body of cosmological force. Humans have inherited their biology from the chemistry of the environment, and have inherited an animating soul from a cosmological force.

The first two humans were made by the god with an innate fault of disobedience that separated them from their first father. Since then all humans have been sexually reproduced. Humans have not come from the body of a god as they are in general crude and lacking in intelligence. The Christian birth story of the superior son of a human-like god is a crude metaphor that relegates all other humans to be inferior. The Christian story obscures a profound truth of existence; life comes from the body of the earth and a triune soul force is a continuation of a body of cosmological force. The human soul is not related to a good human-like god but is a continuation of a cosmological force as the triune soul force of hunger, sex and reproduction, and aggression.

An eternal unchanging human-like god is a humanly conceived nostrum, an antidote to the scourge of merciless shifting and uncertain moments of time. The vandal of time has no mercy and brings ruin to everything. Possessions and relationships continually change in the water-like wake, a sequence of all-eroding time. Humans attend religious services as they have a deeply felt metaphysical need to touch an unchanging eternal realm. Like light that consists of discrete photon particles, time consists of points of now moments that arrive and depart. Light flows as wave lengths while time flows as a seamless connected series of changing cause and effect events. Time is relative to humans and life, relative to the environment, and all time is relative motion of an ever dynamic nonlocal cosmological force. The human body erodes during life. The triune soul force of hunger for food, sex and reproduction, and aggression bring continual changing experiences of life, but as a continuation of a cosmological force, do not erode with the changes of time. The human triune soul force is resilient enough to survive physical death.

Free Will And Effort

It has been observed and commented on that there exists in living forms what is called a "will to live." Willing is an effort to exist, to function, have, to do, pulling, holding, having, and letting go. This phenomenon occurs as a continuation of a non-phenomenon, a non-appearing ground. Just as life is a continuation of the earth and is supported by rock layers and soil of the ground, so too is the environment a continuation of and is supported by a cosmological ground. The attempt and effort to exist and live inside is supported by what is outside. Life is a continuation of a supporting environment that is a continuation of a supporting cosmological force. Willing of life consists of relative movement and effort dependent on an environment and so is never free.

The human sense of a "free will" derives in part from ignorance of relative dependent conditions of the environment and limitations of biology. The other sense of a free will is the dimly sensed and vague perception, the ineffable and unarticulated sensing of the triune soul force. Individual life is a continuation of a limitless nonlocal cosmological force that interconnects with and moves all that exists of the environment and living forms through space and time dimensions. This explains the individual sensing of a free will, rather than the childish mythological story of Middle East and Western religions and the dogmatic assertions of St. Augustine (354-430 CE).

All living forms share a subconscious soul as a triune force that compels hunger for food, sex and/or reproduction, and aggression, while the conscious sense of self varies with species and individual development. The "self" will to live and exist consists of conscious willing actions to survive. In contrast the "soul" will to live and exist is the predominant subconscious willing effort of cells and organs to function. The relative efforts of hunger for food, sex and reproduction, and aggression, grow the life form as a continuation of a cosmological force.

Beyond observation of behaviors of the physical environment and living forms, a metaphysical origin in popular thinking is identified as a human-like god. In reality, there is a cosmological force that moves relative forces of electromagnetism and gravity, and quanta of atoms and electrons of elements, and the environment of stars, galaxies, suns, moons, and planets into, through and out of existence. Existence is not the result of a human-like god but an effort of cosmological force of cause and effect.

Theists think of human behaviors of eating, sex and reproduction, and aggression as evils of the flesh as opposed to the fantastically magnified moral and ethical goodness of a human-like god. These condemned and controlled human behaviors are in truth a triune soul force existing as a continuation of the environment and a cosmological force. Impaired by ignorance, humans think of sex as only a physical act and do not to see that it has a primary metaphysical origin. Sex brings forth life only as an active continuation of the local environment and a nonlocal cosmological force.

The rat race of life is to do, accomplish, and to have. In contrast, the traditional "spiritual" life is to reduce the cloying for food, to reduce, moderate, and eventually remove the craving for sex, and to reduce acts of aggression. The reduction of these triune soul forces has always been how an individual gets beyond the lower and vulgar human condition and is how to rise to an improved or higher level of existence. When conscious attention and effort is directed to observing and studying the triune soul force, an individual can gradually see beyond changing sensations and subconscious habitual behavior patterns of eating, sex, and aggression.

The triune soul moves the body and has evolved the brain to produce images or pictures from sensations. Sensations of the senses and images or pictures of the brain are driven to function by the triune force of the soul to survive. Since the conscious and subconscious effort to exist is a continuation of a cosmological force, individual willing continues until trained to relax the triune soul force. The triune soul force is a continuation of a cosmological force, and therefore survives the death of the body. Cosmological law of conservation of energy, mass, and momentum, saves the essence of an individual rather than a human-like god savior.

Conservation

Relative motion is axiomatic, and all that moves must therefore be a continuation of some greater cosmological force. The environment and life is contained in the relative container of space and time, as a continuation of an uncontained cosmological force. Thought cannot perceive and is not capable of measuring a nonlocal cosmological force, and can only infer it. Therefore of necessity, most humans must measure an unmeasurable force by utilizing what is most familiar, a human-like first father located as first in a time sequence of human reproduction. This is the human way of rationalizing an irrational origin, of measuring what is an unmeasurable beginning. Rather than a first-hand perceiving of a beginning, there is only a second-hand conceiving of a human-like first father god.

Fear generates a need for knowing the protection of a god in a difficult to protect life existence, and what protects humans must necessarily be known as human-like. Humans must also be preserved and survive physical death, and what preserves humans must be a human-like actor. In reality what preserves humans is not only external but is also internal. There is no external first parent that breathed life into humans and made all other respiring life. What preserves is both outside and inside of humans, outside as a multidimensional nonlocal cosmological force, and inside as a continuation of it as the triune soul force. There is a continuation from a cosmological force to the environment and to the immanent function of living forms. The subconscious soul force is reflected in conscious emotions and thoughts to obtain food and eat, to have sex and reproduce, and to be aggressive. At the time of physical death some degree of human self-conscious awareness is conserved as a continuation of the subconscious soul force, the environment, and a cosmological force.

Based on the law of conservation, energy is conserved during conversion from one state to another and thereby remains constant. The law of conservation of mass states that the total mass of an isolated system is not reduced by any interaction and change of its parts. The change of any mass is always equal to the mass of its products. The laws of conservation state that something must remain of any relative process. The product at the time of physical death consists of not only atoms and electrons of elements but also a triune soul force no longer located in a physical and energy mass. A lifetime of effort as the willing to exist and live, of acquiring and consuming food, having sex and reproducing, and acts of aggression, are forces to be preserved. Body mass ends and elements of energy disperse in death but the products of this change continue as a conserved force and dimensional momentum.

Jewish Error

The Jewish peoples conceived their Semitic origin to be a human-like god and first father of many generations of human fathers (Genesis 5, 10). They did not see their origin as coming from a long evolution of differing human species, chimps, mammals, and environment. The Jews also did not consider their origin as making something special inside of them as an immanent "soul." They believed there was no soul but a shadow-like remainder of life. After physical death, both good and evil persons went under the earth to the pit of Sheol. For the Jews a sin or separation occurred, when in their effort to find caring on an uncaring earth, they imagined the beginning of existence to be a human-like first father in a sequence of biological fathers. This was the Jewish way of finding care in an uncaring environment. The psychological construct of a human-like god is the separating and sinful failure to recognize humans to be a continuation of the environment and a cosmological force.

Hebrew for the English word "spirit" is ruah, meaning wind or air, and in humans is the animating process of breathing and speaking. The human-like god did not breathe "the breath of life" into any other life form, only the first human as mentioned in Genesis 2:5. The Hebrew word erroneously translated into English as soul is "nephesh," which means alive or a "living creature." The word is used in the Old Testament for both animals and humans. In Genesis 1:20-21 the word nephesh is used for ocean animals, in Genesis 1:24 for land animals, in Genesis 1:30 for both birds and land animals. In Genesis 2:7 the word is also used to refer to the first man as a nephesh, as a living creature or alive.

The Jewish peoples continue to be deluded about what happens after physical death. The Hebrew word for the afterlife is Sheol, meaning "pit," said to be a large dark cavern beneath the earth. To Sheol went the nonphysical part of humans that survived physical death. This nonphysical part is known by the noun "rapa," translated into English as "shade," an allusion to an individual's physical shadow cast on the ground. The "shade" of the deceased that once reflected as a dark shadow on the surface, went down to join the ever darkness under the earth. The word for the nonphysical surviving part of a human "rapa" in Hebrew literally means as a verb "to sink or go down." The surviving part of all deceased, both good and evil, went down to Sheol. Here the individual "shade or shadow" remained until the living no longer remembered them, and they then faded into the darkness of oblivion never to be seen again. It is also interesting to note that the human-like god of the Jews did not dwell in the afterlife, a non-rewarding and non-punishing place located under the earth. In stark contrast, Christians developed an afterlife in the sky or heaven above the earth and a burning punishing hell under the earth. The human-like first father only dwelled in the heaven above, and Satan the enemy of the god resided under the earth near burning lava.

Metaphor of Evil

The main problem of existence is evil (Hebrew ra') that contributed to "sin" (Hebrew hata, separation) in the Garden of Eden story. In the tale, it was the first humans in a sequence of later generations who caused evil by disobeying parental goodness of a first father. The god cursed and inflicted harm and evil upon the two nascent humans (Genesis 3:14-18). To this day and hour the god has not lifted the curse imposed on the lives of descendent humans. In spite of this, Christians continue to foster the view of a loving father who begot his son Jesus. All other humans are "unbegotten" thus marred and so cursed. The Christian theologian St. Augustine (354-430 CE) used the Genesis story to develop the doctrine of "original sin." Faced with the task of explaining the numerous evils on the earth, Christian theologians emphasized an entity unbegotten and made by the god named Satan.

The Garden of Eden story is a metaphor, a crude unknowing of when a human-like god made animals and humans; there was no hunger, no sexual knowledge and reproduction, and no aggression between the first two humans and other life forms. As the metaphorical story unfolds, the triune soul force is portrayed to be a curse from a god. The curse inflicted is to till the soil to appease hunger, knowledge of human sexuality was obtained by disobediently taking it from a special Tree of Knowledge of Good and Evil, and aggression is portrayed as having a root in envy and jealousy between Cain and Abel.

In their search to find and identify the beginning of existence, the early Jews made up the simplistic story of a human-like god. While the concept of a first father is patently false, there is at least one metaphorical truth in the Genesis story; the fault inside of humans. The fault portrayed is an episode of disobedience that caused a separation between humans and a human-like god. In reality human disobedience is the innate will to live of the triune soul force of hunger for food, sex and reproduction, and aggression. However; the traits cause interpersonal trouble among humans and are deemed ungodly, declared to be a curse from a human-like god.

Asceticism

Hindu seers realized life often consists of undesired and difficult to control experiences. They proceed to develop ascetic practices to reduce what moves the body to act from inside.. Fasting and begging for food controls hunger, celibacy controls sex, and "ahimsa" or non-harming controls aggression. Buddhist monastic rules (patimokkha) deal predominantly with the triune soul force. Monks are required to eat one meal daily before noon, practice celibacy, and compassion is the antidote to aggression.

Similarly, the Christian Rule of St. Benedict has many rules that deal with the triune soul force of hunger for food such as eating only two meals daily, limit of one pound of bread, a "hemina" or half pint or ten ounces of wine with meals, and meat from four-footed animals is prohibited (chapters 35-41). The rule of celibacy is also enforced. A number of chapters discuss the rule of obedience and not displaying aggression toward or hitting fellow monks. In chapter 66 there is mention of appointing a porter to interact with people outside the monastery so that monks can avoid contact with the worldly population, who are unethical, uneducated, and aggressive. The monks are exhorted with these words:

Just as there is an evil zeal of bitterness
Which separates from God and leads to hell,
So there is a good zeal
Which separates from vices and leads to God,
And to everlasting life. (Chapter 72)

The vices are the soul forces that are real while a human-like god is a false conception. These western rules and reference to a human-like god is a rally for humans to a higher attitude by disciplining the triune soul force. By so doing there is hope to reach the "heavenly homeland" (chapter 73) that the human-like god reserves for himself and allows only the worthy and virtuous to enter therein while punishing the wicked.

For the worldly individual, over-eating and overweight, overly obsessed with sex for pleasure or for the results of reproduction, and being overly impatient and aggressive, may certainly contribute to an early death. To obsess and overly indulge in these activities can also be seen as an unwillingness to relinquish this life and is a refusal to peacefully exit and leave the earthly dimension. To learn to discipline, limit, and to reduce the triune soul force is the way to salvation from endless time, is the euthanasia, the "good death" of leaving life existence.

Life is a series of looking for, anticipating, and experiencing pleasures that serve to distract attention from the continual change, errors, and pains of existence. A human-like god is a way of glamorizing earthly life, a way of overlooking and not indulging in what is bad and evil, a way to make life appear better than it is in reality, and a way of glamorizing what happens after life. Very few humans can look upon their own existence and life in general without thinking of a human-like god. Accepting the idea of a human-like god is a shortcut to being optimistic about life, and is how an individual protects his life on the outside from other life forms, from fellow humans, from the environment, from ageing and death and what waits after death as either reward or punishment of oblivion. Pity poor humans who are plagued inside by a lack of sufficient knowledge and an inability to accurately reason, plagued by the triune soul force of hunger for food, sex and reproduction, and aggression. Troubles on both the inside and outside lead to what is considered by theists to be a "special knowledge'; the conception of a human-like god for protection. A god is an imagined and constructed symbol, a supernatural hope for those bereft of natural hope, an imaginary human beacon in the dark helplessness and hopelessness of life and death. The Middle East derived Western god merely reflects the human ego and determination to survive on earth and after death.

To seek for what is good in life and death is to seek for what is human-like. The average person gathers in weekly religious groups seeking the goodness and guidance of a god. Much smaller groups of theistic monks gather in monasteries seeking to comprehend the good of a human-like god. In contrast, nontheistic ascetics seek the good of reducing the triune soul force. Ascetics direct some of their own capacity for aggression toward and against their body and brain so as to reduce and extirpate the triune soul force. They seek to dig up and pull out the roots of individual life that grow inside as a continuation of an outside supporting ground of the earth that in turn grows from the ground of a nonlocal cosmological force.

Humans artistically imagine human-like gods to symbolize the unknown forces, energies, and events of the environment. A non-theist ascetic senses that what has brought him into existence is not a human-like god. He senses the life force inside is a continuation of an outside real cosmological force. He also senses that he does not in any way come from an unreal human-like god based on a theological fiction story. All is tied as time, a series of relative events that move through a space of height, width, and depth; a relative succession ever tied to a timeless cosmological force. An individual life existence is an extension of a non-visible thread woven from the cosmological quantum yarn of "super strings." There is no human-like "weaver" as based on the theistically conceived story yarn of a god, only an ever weaving of super strings.

Worth Knowing

It is worthwhile to know in life that a human-like god resides only in the human brain where it is conceived. A human-like god is believed by many to exist based solely on personal faith. In prescientific and primitive religious literature faith reflects the mental-emotional effort, determination, and tenacity of an individual to be protected in life and after death. A human-like god is an anodyne, a palliative for lower level human behaviors of existence, and for those individuals disoriented in the confusing struggle of making their way through the maze of life. Most of human experience consists of trial and error learning. Intentions for a good or favorable outcome are always accompanied by unintended side effects that are detrimental. This is the sense of irony and fate. Gestalt psychology speaks of a "figure-ground," meaning a foreground and a background. To perceive a foreground the background is of necessity ignored. Likewise in any situation there is the tendency to ignore or disregard at least some of the possible or probable consequences.

No matter how much is consciously learned of any area of knowledge, each individual has to deal with the subconscious background of a triune soul force. Many humans cannot save their health, cannot save themselves financially, and cannot save the deterioration of their relationships. The majority of the human population has gone and continues to go to a human-like god to save themselves and others. The subconscious soul force abetted by conscious knowledge is its own savior and those who do not make the effort to learn about themselves can just go elsewhere. Conscious meditative attention can explore, reduce, and relinquish excessive or deficient subconscious willing of hunger, sex, and aggression. Conscious attention aided by memory has as its task the directing of the individual subconscious soul that is a continuation of a cosmological force. Conscious attention and willing must resolve the triune soul force, a relative part of a great "cosmic go" or cosmological force.

The environment and life are a continuation, not of a human-like god but a cosmological force. The human conscious physical brain must learn about the subconscious metaphysical soul force that exists as a continuation of a cosmological force that moves all. The soul force runs both as a subconscious background and also directs conscious awareness. This poor blend of predominant subconscious and surface conscious attention and awareness finds it difficult to comprehend its origin as a continuation of cosmological force, so the brain fashions a human-like beginning.

In the past there has been a human struggle for knowledge that has resulted in the development of various kinds of stone tools and weapons. In modern times the struggle for knowledge continues to develop better tools and weapons, and also machines of many kinds including cars, aircraft, cell phones, `and computers. The long struggle to obtain knowledge of the origin of existence has resulted in the various conceived notions and writings about a human-like god. Knowledge of physics, biology, and geology, has been developed based on observation, record-keeping and publication of test results. This is in contrast to the non-observation of a human like god that is artistically shaped in religious writings by subjective imagination.

The religious view of a human-like god and the view of a soul have to this day not been realistically examined. Faulty thinking by theologians and non-thinking opinions by the public have been poor substitutes for perception and explanation. The public accepts the subjective conception of a god to be objective and conceives the "soul" of life in a mythic way to be associated with a human-like god. The foolish majority of a population has always accepted poor explanations that have been promulgated by theistic religions.

Science argues that a god and a soul do not exist as both cannot be detected and observed, or empirically tested. Science views both a god and a soul as subjective and conceptual, not ever as objective and perceptual realties. Religion counters the science argument with the claim that a god cannot be detected or observed as it is a spiritual substance that exists only in another dimension. The soul is said to exist in the body and is also a spiritual substance that cannot be detected and observed. Science is correct about the nonexistence of a human-like god but is not correct about the existence of an animating soul.

Self and Soul

Conscious attention of the brain/mind is what is known as the "self," and is capable of reasoning and making choices. Sigmund Freud (1856-1939) conceived of what he called the conscious and unconscious mind; mind being a referent for brain function and awareness. In contradistinction to Freud, the word "self" denotes the conscious personality while the word "soul" denotes the subconscious triune force of hunger, sex, and aggression.

Mythological religious thinking has produced many nonsensical concepts of the soul through years of human existence. The eternal soul is not a thing but is a dynamic force that resides in the movement and growth of viruses and bacteria, multicellular life, and human life. The soul resides in and moves the uniting of sperm and egg cell; it moves the function of cells and organs of the body. The triune soul force of hunger, sex and reproduction, and aggression moves life as a continuation of a cosmological force that moves the cosmos.

It is the human soul that gets out of control. What gets out of control in life is usually not the conscious self but the subconscious soul, the triune force of hunger for food, sex and reproduction, and aggression. This active triune force in all cells and organs enables the body to live and survive. Since the triune soul force is a continuation of a cosmological force, therefore it is not destructible and there is by necessity some sort of dimensional survival. An unknown dimension that transcends the familiar earthly one, is often symbolized by the sky, caves, and religious buildings.

Brain and Body

The philosopher David Hume (1711-1776) wrote, "Reason is, and ought only to be the slave of the passions, and can never pretend to any other office than to serve and obey them." No truer words have been spoken, especially when human brain function is more closely examined.

The human body consists of approximately one hundred trillion cells. For every cell of the body that exists, there are one hundred bacteria, and a rough total of ten thousand trillion bacteria on and in the human body. At birth the human brain weighs approximately four hundred grams or three-quarters of a pound and that of an adult about fifteen hundred grams or three pounds. The brain is only about three percent of total body weight yet is estimated to consume twenty-five percent of nutrients, seventy percent of available glucose, and twenty-five percent of inhaled oxygen.

Based on the best available neuroscience estimate, the human brain consists of some eighty-six billion neurons and approximately the same number of non-neuron or glial cells. Brain glial cells function to surround, support, and insulate neurons from each other, provide oxygen and nutrients, remove dead neurons and destroy infectious pathogens.

The cerebellum or "little brain" is the second largest physical part of the brain. It is located beneath and posterior to the cerebral cortex and controls body movement, motor learning, coordination, equilibrium, and posture. The cerebellum also performs some cognitive functions of regulating attention, sensory perception, emotional responses, and language. The main area for body movement occurs in the cerebellum, with other areas located in the cerebral cortex. The small premotor and motor area of the cerebral cortex provides conscious feedback and guidance for the subconscious cerebellum that regulates movement and balance. The muscles involved retain some sort of motor neuron memory that when repeated becomes subconscious habit. Muscle memory consists of a specific muscular behavior stored as memory through repetition as a physiological adaptation to repetitive physical behavior that increases neuromuscular ability and control. Repeated movement creates muscle memory and enables the behavior to be accomplished without conscious attention to the developed skill. A few examples of muscle memory are skateboarding, surfing, riding a bicycle, driving a car, and playing a musical instrument.

Neuroscience research has determined that the cerebral cortex weighs an average of approximately 1250 grams and is eighty-two percent of brain mass. The cerebellum weighs approximately 150 grams and is ten percent of brain mass. The midbrain consisting of the thalamus, hypothalamus, amygdala, and hippocampus make up another 100 grams and eight percent of brain mass.

Of the total number of eighty-six billion brain neurons, the cerebral cortex as the predominant reasoning area of the brain, consists of only sixteen billion neurons, with the left hemisphere containing somewhat more neurons than the right hemisphere. In contrast, the cerebellum that regulates body movement and posture consists of sixty-nine billion neurons, and the midbrain that regulates subconscious autonomic sympathetic and parasympathetic functions of the body account for roughly one billion neurons for an approximate seventy billion midbrain neurons. Only nineteen percent or sixteen billion of the total eighty-six billion brain neurons are possibly utilized for reasoning, and the other eighty-one percent or seventy billion serve to regulate the one hundred trillion cells of the body. There are four times more brain neurons that regulate body functions than are utilized for reasoning. It is therefore quite obvious that the subconscious triune soul force of hunger for food, sex and reproduction, and aggression, innate in one hundred trillion cells of the body and midbrain, easily overwhelm the conscious reasoning of the cerebral cortex.

The evolved human cerebral cortex of the brain consists of roughly sixteen billion neurons of which neuroscience estimates that only from one percent (one hundred million) to ten percent (one billion six hundred thousand) cells are consciously aware at any waking moment. The other parts of the brain, the cerebellum and midbrain, consist of seventy billion neurons that regulate subconscious autonomic body functions such as digestion, heartbeat, posture, and respiration. The minor conscious self of reasoning brain cells have the onerous task of moderating individual life but become easily overwhelmed by the major subconscious triune soul force of hunger, sex, and aggression.

Ways Of Knowing

There are three ways of knowing objects. In reality they are distinct but overlap each other. Objects are known through sensations of seeing, hearing, smelling, tasting, and touching. The primal way of knowing is stimulus-response of willing behavior, for an object or against it, attraction or antipathy, as thought, emotion, or immediate and non-reflective body movement directed to the object.

The second way of knowing brings many benefits and also much harm to humankind. Coequal with willing, an evolved brain has the further ability to reason about an object; measure it, analyze it, and to using willing technical behaviors to shape it. This has become the way of tool-making of modern science, trial and error testing and learning.

The third way is not to willfully seek to have or be aggressive toward an object, or not to reason about or to measure or analyze it, but instead to pause and to ponder the object. This includes being aesthetically sensitive to an object, to feel its intimate presence, to wonder about it as a way to know it, to let it fill attention so as to become one with it. This is the way of meditation and intuition. This third way of knowing is also that of an artist who perceives, albeit vaguely, a dynamic of reality and then conceives a work of art to direct attention to it.

Meditation

During a focus of attention known as meditation, the electrical activity of the brain is reduced from a waking beta wave frequency of 13-30 hertz or cycles per second, to an alpha wave frequency of 8-13 hertz that relaxes the autonomic nervous system, lowers blood pressure, heart rate, and stress hormones. Theta brain waves have a frequency of 4-7 hertz, and produce deeper relaxation and enhance creativity. Delta wave frequency of 0.5-4 hertz occurs mainly during dreamless sleep. Gamma brain waves were first detected in the 1960's and have been later confirmed to oscillate between 25-40 hertz and have been detected up to 100 hertz. Gamma brain waves function to synchronize various parts of the brain, beginning in the midbrain thalamus and radiate to the back of the brain and from there to the front of the brain 40 times per second.

Meditation focuses attention which reduces distraction of sensations through the senses, and calms brain image-making. Meditation fixes attention and reaches a poise in sensate now moments. With meditation practice through consistent effort there occurs better observation of body sensations, and comprehension of the triune willing force of hunger for food, sex, and aggression. Meditatively stilling the secondary images of the brain/mind, an individual can come to better see the primary soul force of the body.

The cerebral cortex has evolved in time and may have been preceded by earlier midbrain structures and body organs. The cerebral neurons make images inside the brain of now sensations of sight, sound, smell, taste, and touch of what is outside, and makes images of past and future. Midbrain neurons that regulate the body, also direct cerebral neurons to generate images and reasoning so as to obtain food, sex, and act with aggression. The brain neurons of image-making and of reasoning, are much less in number compared to the neurons of autonomic body functions. The essence of individual existence is not cerebral images of now, past, and future, but midbrain neurons for cell and organ body functions.

Neuroscience research has found that typically from one and at the most ten percent of cerebral brain function is conscious. Conversely it has been estimated that ninety-nine to ninety percent of total brain function is subconscious. Average attention span is estimated to be as brief as three seconds and perhaps up to ten seconds unless focused on a prolonged learning task. Gestalt psychology theory says that attention is continually shifting perception between figure and ground, in other words attention attends to what is foreground and the rest of the environment recedes to the background.

Each brain neuron is estimated to have some one thousand synapses with other neurons. Brain storage capacity has been estimated to range from one terabyte to one hundred terabytes, and even three petabytes, or three thousand million million bytes of data capacity. This is a lot of data capacity.

The word "mind" is a noun referent that refers to the conscious and subconscious activity of the brain. A human "motive" is what motion and change is tied to as subject and object, motion inside and outside. Consciousness or the quality of knowing is split into conscious and subconscious, and into subject and object of inside and outside.

Conscious Subject > Object
Subconscious

Humans "see" with use of the physical eyes, and with conscious visual brain images of now sensations, memory images, future images, and subconscious seeing of dream images. To see is also to perceive and then to conceive concepts or ideas, and to comprehend. Sensations of a biological existence develop in the brain as subconscious perceptions, and conscious conceptions of reasoning and measuring. Much of the cerebral brain's job is to make images of sensations from the senses of what is outside, and images of past and future. The cerebrum or cerebral brain also consciously measures, compares, or reasons using numbers to estimate size, distance, time, and to shape images. In contrast, the soul has no image making capacity and does not reason, the soul is a triune force within the body that grows and moves. The triune soul of hunger for food, sex and reproduction, and aggression is evolutionarily prior to the evolved ability for image-making.

The cerebral cortex of the brain is where a human-like god is conceived and is where a god resides as a concept and nowhere else. What is conceived as giving the first impetus to life from the outside is said to be a god, and the impetus for life inside is conceived to be a "soul" made by the god. In reality there exists outside only a cosmological force that moves all things into, through and out of dimensional existence. Inside of living forms there is a continuation of cosmological force as a triune soul force. Inside single cell bacteria, plants, animals and humans, there is a forcefully felt need for nourishment, reproduction, and aggression. A soul is the impetus and act of living as the triune force of hunger to ingest food, engage in sex and reproduction, and act with aggression.

Sensations of the senses to the cerebral brain constructs images of an outside now environment, constructs past images and imagined future images. The will to exist and live of the triune soul force of hunger, sex and reproduction, and aggression, stimulates images derived from changing sensations. Through a practice of a focus of attention and concentration, an individual through realizing that images consist of ever changing sensations, can deconstruct the flowing stream of brain images. With discipline, the soul force is reduced from interest in pulling one way or another.

Through consistent practice and effort of attention directed to observation of calming the brain/mind image-making and emotions, then body function and parts can be explored. With practice, conscious attention can better observe body function and subconscious hunger for food, sex and reproduction, and aggression of the will-to-live. Conscious observation leads to the comprehension that the conscious and subconscious function and willing of the body is a continuation of a cosmological force.

Meditation slows the image-making process of the cerebral brain and focuses attention more completely on "now" moments. Moderation and balance can then be achieved. Comprehension of the triune soul to be a continuation of a cosmological force leads to the discarding of the popular but false conceptual belief of a human-like god. Rather than live observantly of now moments of changing sensations, the average person lives in a non-observant pattern of subconscious habit-memory of eating food, engaging in sex and reproduction, and aggression.

Leaning how to meditate is not easy. Sitting and focusing attention, the average person may become annoyed, painfully bored, and easily distracted, or soon tires and drifts into sleep. A non-meditating person becomes vulnerable to dream-like associative thinking, to media suggestion of all kinds, and to peer pressure of family and friends. Conditioned by inattention waking dreams ensue, difficult if not impossible to awake from. Also attendant to habitual inattention are many afflictions of addictions and psychological disorders.

The ability to focus attention results in an ability to magnify now moments and subtle details become more noticeable as dreamy associations are curtailed and replaced by intuitive perceptions. Jaded conceptions fade and are replaced by pristine perceptions of reality experience. Reducing conscious images of remembering and imagining leads to awareness of subconscious content of suppressed and repressed memory and imaginations, so that clarity dawns. When conscious attention can better focus, the subconscious content of willing is revealed to consist of a triune soul force of hunger, sex, and aggression that is further perceived to be a continuation of a cosmological force.

Life

The triune soul force need for nourishment develops following conception. Sex and the ability to reproduce eventually develops. In the year 2000 the age for sexual maturity occurred on average between eleven to thirteen years for both sexes. The ability for aggression comes with increasing maturity and muscle development. By the age of eighteen both males and females are eligible for military service.

In contrast to the triune soul force, the findings of modern neuroscience is that brain maturity occurs much later at around twenty-five years of age. The primary sexual functions of brain and body and muscular aggression mature much earlier than that of cerebral reasoning ability. Conscious learning and knowing contribute to individual survival, yet is secondary to the primary subconscious will to live of hunger for food, sex and reproduction, and aggression. The triune soul force is located in every organ and cell of the body. Each cell wants nourishment, wants to reproduce or replicate, and wants to aggressively grow and live.

The essence of living cells is the metaphysical will to live. Without some kind of intentional effort, life would not exist. The intentional effort has been projected beyond life and the environment to the imagined intention and effort of a human-like god. The intentional effort of the will to live of a single cell to multicellular life requires support and is a continuation of the environment. Life is an outgrowth of the environment, and the earth is formed from energy particles and relative forces, and these are a direct continuation of a cosmological force.

Each individual has entered the foray of life consisting of a series of semi-orderly events inserted with errors. The path of individual life is a continuing struggle of making choices. Certainty is often uncertain and so, the crux of life is the problem of choice. Humans often ignore what needs to be done and do what should not be done; difficult to tell the difference. Each individual likes or dislikes, and approves or disapproves of other's choices. So be it. Love is touted by many to be the answer to the problems of life. Relationships can be supportive and pleasurable but regardless of how much someone loves or is loved, they must deal with their own and others unreasoning triune soul force. For the triune soul there are three kinds of love; love for food, love for sex and reproduction, and love for aggression.

The problem of life is that there are two predominant poles of experience, sought for pleasure and unsought for pain. From both the individual learns to not overly cling to passing pleasures and to better avoid as much as prudently possible, the often unavoidable reality of pain. Affinity begets its twin of dis-affinity, evident in any social milieu as attraction and antipathy.

Life in general a frustrating experience. Frustration is defined as "an emotional response to the hindering or preventing of a potential satisfying activity." Human life is synonymous with frustration that comes not from a human-like god but from receiving less of what is wanted or more of what is unwanted. Humans get the frustration of unwanted illnesses, accidents, and relationships. Ascetics, monks, and spiritual aspirants remove themselves from the frustrations of everyday life, so as to focus attention and better comprehend life and its origin. Even an average individual may come to comprehend the truth, that life is predominantly a condition of frustration.

Life is an irritation, defined as "an inflammatory reaction of the body, an excessive or painful stimulus, annoyance, and troubling thoughts or emotions." Life is irritated with what is, and is irritated with what isn't. Each individual finds ample conscious and subconscious irritation from what exists in now moments, by memories and emotions of the past, and irritation as fear of what will or will not occur in the future. The average person seeks relief from the irritations of life by indulging in food, sex, and aggression. Theists turn from what irritates them to an imagined god for relief or to at least to reduce if not remove the many irritations of human life. Theists also lighten the irritations of life by looking forward to a non-irritating and rewarding afterlife of heaven while hoping to avoid the irritating punishments of a hell.

A popular saying is, "God helps those who help themselves." The reverse also applies, if the person does not help himself the god will not help. Since the person is the origin of any particular conceived human-like god, then the concept is only helpful if the person makes use of it to rise higher in life by helping themselves. A god is an imaginary mediator and protector of humans, a mental model to reduce and transcend both outside and inside conflict. The model of a good and merciful god is held up to conscious attention as an object located outside. What easily diverts attention from an outside imaginary human-like god is the real inside triune soul force, a direct continuation of an all-powerful cosmological force.

The question must be asked, is the earth and life "made" for human happiness? The answer of most religions is a resounding no! No human-like god has ever directed or commanded humans to just go forth on the earth and "have fun" in life. If a human-like god were sensitive, empathetic, concerned, and protective, like a human parent is for their children, then that god would feel much pain and be nauseated by what occurs to humans on a daily basis. No human-like god has ever sought nor seeks to relieve and protect humans from suffering. Instead the dry concept of a human-like god stands by only as an inert artistically imagined and erected mental statue gradually ruining with the passage of time.

Jewish theism tells the story of how the ground and humans were cursed by the human-like god (Genesis 3) and how most of life was destroyed in a flood (Genesis 6-8). The book of Ecclesiastes states that "A good name is better than precious ointment; and the day of death than the day of one's birth" (7:1). The message of Christianity as portrayed by the life of Jesus is that even the godly will suffer and die painfully, and that only the cult of anticipating and accepting death can take away the suffering of life. The religion of Islam declares the "jihad" of military struggle and war and the killing of any infidels who disagree with its teachings. Use of the word jihad, meaning military combat, occurs one hundred-sixty four times in the Quran. Modern Muslims also speak of an interior jihad; the individual struggle to maintain faith in the delusion of a good human-like god.

In Hinduism the origin of all things including the many gods is Brahman, a nonhuman transcendent force that cannot be appealed to and that operates through the law of karma or cause and effect to move each individual through cycles of reincarnation. The Hindu god Shiva is popularly portrayed in art as "Nataraja," meaning, "Lord of the Cosmic Dance," symbolizing the dancing animating motion of the environment and life. Shiva is also symbolized by the lingam-yoni, the male and female genitals, and this artwork symbolizes the dance of sex and reproduction that ends in the fast or slow ageing and destruction of death. Buddha taught "sabbe sankhara dukkha" that all willing behavior of life is suffering as it consists of parts. Buddha also taught the law and necessity of karma or cause and effect change and recurring lives of rebirth.

Even the scientific theory of evolution echoes with the refrain "survival of the fittest." Yet contemplating this truth of life for a while, attention and thoughts become strained. Many in life may seek relief by imaginatively daydreaming about something good and comforting, such as a human-like god.

Comprehension

The great mystery sought to be solved by many is how and to what the individual is connected to as an origin. Pondering to perceive and comprehend what moves the universe, an individual may study the environment and living forms. Eventually though, an individual may be curious enough to observe and investigate his own interior. An individual may withdraw from the many busy distractions of life to meditate, to reduce distraction of sensations of the senses, to observe and calm the brain picture-making of images. Then an insightful individual will come to observe and to see how the triune soul is a continuation of a cosmological force that moves all.

The few wise of the species have through meditation sought to disentangle the dynamic of individual personality and to communicate details of a method to transform an individual life. The wise of many cultures have sought to awake from the daily dream of an all too often painful life existence. Individuals with varying ability and degrees of success have struggled to perceive and to comprehend the mystery of the environment, and the human body and cognitive functions. The eventual solution consists of a series of intuitive leaps across a chasm to reach clear apperception.

The solution to the problem of life has necessitated a practice to fix attention for an extended time, and in this way develop intuitive perception. Meditation was utilized to observe that sensations of the senses are transformed into pictures in the brain, and it was observed how these are consciously used to reason and to conceive concepts and ideas. The next and almost impassable and prodigious leap was to perceive how these secondary conscious mental processes are related to the primary subconscious triune soul force. This was achieved through ascetic practices such as fasting, celibacy, and compassion. The next great leap was to perceive how the body, brain, and environment are a continuation of a cosmological force. This was not so easy to accomplish, for in the effort to leap across a space of unknowing, to comprehend the origin of existence, most individuals lacked both strength and determination. They fell into a conceptual chasm of theistic myths about a human-like god.

Better success to penetrate the phenomenal puzzle of existence and annunciate an answer was achieved only over a span of many years by two percipient individuals; Buddha (circa 623-543 BCE) of India and the philosopher Arthur Schopenhauer (1788-1860). These two individuals, each in their own way, managed the heroic feat of comprehending that a human-like god is merely an artistically imagined first parent having a utilitarian function. Though not specifically stated, each in their own way also comprehended that what animates human life of body and brain is the triune soul force. Others may have accomplished this numinous feat, yet they remain unknown.

A halo, nimbus, or aureole, is a circular or rounded radiant light, usually golden, yellow, or white, that often surrounds the head of an individual in religious art to portray a special or higher knowledge. The Greek Titan god Helios, said to drive the chariot of the sun across the sky, is portrayed with a human-like body and a halo surrounding his head. Later Christian artists portray Jesus and Christian saints with a halo surrounding their heads. This iconography is of a special light of knowledge that radiates from within the person. The light-radiating illusionary knowledge of a human-like god is based only on subjectively conceived knowledge, not on objectively observed knowledge. In Leonardo da Vinci's well-known work, the *Last Supper*, painted 1495-1497, Jesus and his followers are portrayed without halos. Leonardo's obvious artistic comment through the painting is that all humans are natural, and as such a human-like god is a subjectively conceived natural idea.

In contrast to western theistic art, the nontheistic Buddha is often portrayed with a halo, symbolizing subjective psychological awareness of objective observed realities. Usually portrayed sitting, his eyes are near closed or closed to reduce attention to sensations from outside. With the brain/mind not organizing sensations to construct now images, past and future images are also calmed. Functions inside the body are observed to be a continuation of what is outside. The triune soul is the inside cause of the calamity of life, while the environment is the outside cause of calamity. To arrive near the pinnacle potential of human development is to reach a level of peace and serenity. The arrived at peace pertains to both an outside aesthetic and tranquil environment and on the inside as health, and freedom from the triune soul force. The individual may also develop the peace of the heightened extrasensory ability of knowing, such as clairvoyance and other enhanced intuitive abilities of knowledge and wisdom.

Whoever seeks comprehension and wisdom seeks to be enlightened, to bring the conscious light of intuitive perception and illuminate what is hidden in subconscious darkness. It will long be hidden from most humans that the conception of a human-like god is an imaginative and artistic expression with a utilitarian function. It will also be long hidden that the phenomenon of life consists of a triune soul force that is a continuation of the earth environment, and a cosmological force that pervades multiple dimensions.

Escape

While not obvious at first glance, potential or actual pain is the substratum of life existence. The only way out is a progression of a gradual or sudden shift to a relieving change of pleasure. Throughout life there are continuing efforts to have pleasurable experience, to remember past pleasures, or to imagine future pleasures. Pain intensifies for living forms until a change is made, for example, after a prolonged sitting posture, the change of the body from the discomfort and pain of sitting to standing is pleasurable. The pain of hunger precedes seeking of food for the pleasure of eating. The hormonal physical and emotional discomfort and pain of sexual frustration and loneliness precedes seeking the pleasure of sexual experience. Life is a continual moving away from the clutches of discomfort and pain and into a relieving state of pleasure. Small pleasures are always better than big pleasures, and knowing how to move out of pain to experience moderate pleasures is the art of living.

Life is the continual restless movement to escape from and to be temporarily free from potential and immediate pain by a transition into pleasure. The escape from or alleviation of the discomfort and pain of excess physical and mental activity is the relieving change to the pleasure of rest. The escape from the discomfort and pain of ignorance is the relieving pleasure of learning. The escape from the discomfort and pain of routine boredom is the relieving pleasure of change and new stimulating interests. The escape from the discomfort and pain of poverty is the relieving change and pleasure of money obtained from work. The escape from the discomfort and pain of physical weakness is the relieving pleasure of change to fitness through exercise and strength. The escape from the painful conditions of life can be the gradual or sudden relieving pleasure of change to death.

The escape from or alleviation of the discomfort and pain of overpopulation, poor economy, or limited territory, is often a relieving change of behavior to the ironically less painful pleasure of armed conflict and war. Then the escape from the excruciating discomfort and pain of conflict and war is the relieving pleasure of peace. So the cycle ever continues, the irrational subconscious seeking to avoid pain and to obtain and experience pleasure is barely tempered by the conscious rational brain/mind. The avoidance of pain and the seeking for pleasure both consciously and subconsciously, is henceforth the great play of life in obtaining food, sex and reproduction, and aggression.

Biblical humans are said to be separate from "good" identified to be a "god" and first father. A human-like god made the environment, life, and humans, proclaimed that it "was good" and that all was "very good" (Genesis 1:25, 31) This godly pronouncement ignores a real observation that life kills and consumes life. A human-like god as a creator of good is but a poor artistic sketch by the human brain and hand. The artistic portrayal of a human-like god as the origin of good, is in reality a loud lament of Semitic experience of what is "not good." What is not good is not godly; the evil pains of life, hunger, sex and reproduction, aggression, ageing, and death.

In the biblical Garden of Eden tale, a human-like god created a life of exclusive pleasure for the first humans. There was no pain of hunger, sex and reproduction, or aggression. The paradise state of pleasure followed by a sequence of secondary pain as portrayed in the myth is a reversal of reality. In reality pain is primal and pleasure is secondary and provides relief. Only from human disobedience did the secondary experience of pain come about through obtaining the inferior knowledge of both good and evil. The god-like knowledge is also the poignant human awareness that reasoning ability is inadequate and often ineffective when confronting the triune soul force of hunger for food, sex and reproduction, and aggression. This is reflected in three main episodes. The first incident of eating the fruit from the Tree of Knowledge of Good and Evil is a concern for hunger, while the second is knowledge of nudity, sex, and the begetting of offspring. The third episode is aggression between the two sons that brought the first human death.

The Garden of Eden story is a literary myth, yet the content of the tale is real knowledge that pain is an evil that is the primary basis of life, and that the good of pleasure is only secondary. Humans obtained knowledge of how to will both, the good of pleasure and the evil of pain. The events in the myth lament the fact that there is more pain in life and less pleasure, and that there is continual transition from pain to pleasure and to pain again. Whatever pleasure is sought, upon attainment is not lasting, and fades into an experience of pain.

Ascetics see that life is a progression from having to not having, and from pain to pleasure and inevitably back to pain again. They practice the reduction of desires for food, sex and reproduction, and aggression. Instead they contemplate a transcendental dimension of experience; in the West a human-like god and in the East what Hindus refer to as "moksha" and the Buddhists as "nirvana."

Twice Born

A Hindu Brahmin boy of seven or eight years old traditionally went through an initiation ritual referred to as "upanayana." The Sanskrit term refers to seeing closely and learning the Vedas, the oldest extant religious writings. Prior to commencing his study of sacred knowledge, the young boy during a ritual was given a hand-woven white cotton thread consisting of three symbolic strands by his guru, after which the boy was recognized to be "twice born." The first birth is biological from the mother, while the "second birth" is a psychological transition to study writings including the Upanishads and yoga teachings that discuss the origin of existence. The studies include the beginning and ending of life, how the inside of the body and brain/mind is connected to the outside, and how to be connected to others. This is metaphysics and ethics as one interest.

Buddha teaches a second way of living with his emphasis on turning away from a busy household life of toil, sex, social conflict and aggression of crime and war, to live a "forest life." In solitary meditation the individual can better observe the workings of body and brain/mind, and can learn to discipline hunger for food, sex and reproduction, and aggression. The lifestyle of forest meditation is a change from an interest in biological mundane daily life to a psychological interest in learning how body and brain function and where life comes from.

Jesus the founder of the Christian religion insists that an individual must be "born again" (John 3:3). In the Greek language "metanoia" literally meaning to think beyond, to see and to comprehend how the physical is a continuation of the metaphysical, and to turn from a lower worldly attitude or "spirit" to a higher and good "Spirit" of inquiry and learning. Yet Jesus obscured reality when he anthropomorphized the outside animating "Spirit" of life to be a first father and human-like god when in reality it is a cosmological force. Not created by a human-like god, the human "spirit" inside humans is the evolved ability to reason, while the "soul" does not reason and is a troubling triune force that is a continuation of a cosmological force.

Christians see hunger for food, sex and reproduction, and aggression as lower original sins, and these appetites of the flesh are to be denied in favor of a higher first father. The sciences of biology and psychology consider these functions to be physical drives and instincts. Hindus and Buddhists see hunger, sex, and aggression as physical forces that must be disciplined as they are a continuation of a metaphysical cosmological force. Being "twice born," or the transition from living a limited mundane physical life of daily economic survival, to a learning discipline and study of a metaphysical reality, is a contributing cause of social caste differences in Hinduism. Being twice born also contributes to the Buddhist practice of forest seclusion from society. Christians may withdraw from profane society to practice monastic living and to study biblical writings. While intended to inspire, the literature is vaguely written and fails to present any method to become twice born.

Theistic religion is a primitive and clumsy cognitive attempt to explain where the environment and life has come from, by use of a human-like god. In contrast, philosophy and its offspring, psychology, is the investigation of such religious views. From a psychological perspective, the conception of a human-like god is an artistic imaginative utilitarian function. Philosophical meditative study reveals that life consists of a triune soul force that is a continuation of the earth environment, in turn a continuation of a multidimensional cosmological force. Not having an interest and lacking time, prompt the majority of humankind to accept a shortcut false view of their existence from a human-like first father god. Yet an intelligent greater creator is objectively unreal and exists only in the subjective artistic imagination of humans.

Spirit

The Latin word "spiritus" means breath and to breathe. The term has been used in the past and continues to be utilized to mean that which is inside and animates humans to live and breathe. The word is also used to mean a greater unseen Spirit from which comes the breath of life. Those who meet in theistic religious groups seek to raise their own lower "spirit" or attitude, to a higher Spirit. Raising to a higher Spirit means only to actuate individual potential to a higher level. In reality, rising from a lower to a higher Spirit occurs only with an effort of learning, from a lower attitude of knowing to a higher knowledge.

In theistic religions a speaker seeks to raise the lower spirit/attitude and behavior of those assembled with a sermon or lecture. The officiant acts as a purveyor of higher knowledge and acts as mediator for a higher Spirit or human-like god. In reality the speaker is only encouraging individuals to elevate their own spirits with the idea of a higher Spirit or god so as to increase their own potential for learning, and to inspire them to rise to a higher potential. The concept of a higher Spirit and human-like god is held before conscious attention for the sole subjective goal to actualize and to live a higher thinking and behaving life. Human reasoning ability of the cerebral cortex conceives and projects a greater reasoning Spirit of a human-like god outside. It also conceives and projects the unreasoning cerebellum and midbrain functions of hunger, sex, and aggression to the outside to be an unhuman, animal-like spirit of evil, a Devil portrayed with horns, tail, and hooves. The unreasoning and devilish opposing environment is also associated with the evil persona.

Sigmund Freud (1856-1939) advocated both a conscious and unconscious mind. Neuroscience has not discovered a mind but has found there is a partial conscious brain and central nervous system and a predominant subconscious brain and autonomic nervous system. Religion uses its own language; it advocates both a human conscious spirit and a soul but fails to adequately define these terms. In reality a human "spirit" is the evolved conscious ability of the brain to reason and think. A soul is a subconscious triune force of hunger for food, sex and reproduction, and aggression. The human spirit of evolved reasoning bolsters existential fear and loneliness by falsely conceiving a greater "Spirit" as the reasoning ability of a human god who, like a puppeteer, dictates plans for humans.

The religious term "spirit" refers to an evolved human ability for conscious reasoning and intuition and extrasensory perception. Conscious ability of reasoning conflicts with the subconscious soul. It is the task of the evolved human conscious spirit of reasoning to resolve the many subconscious conflicts caused by the unreasoning triune soul.

At the time of physical death, the soul essence will be saved by default based on the universe's laws of conservation of mass, energy, and momentum, and "quantum entanglement." There will continue to survive and exist some of the conscious spirit supported by the subconscious soul force, in turn supported by a multi-dimensional reality of a nonlocal cosmological force.

Religious Building

Built for the purpose of worshiping a human-like god, a religious building has meanings other than those consciously intended. One unintended abstract meaning is that the building as a sacred place, is a symbol for the overvalued ego of humans, and of how they are favored as a species on earth by their very own special human-like god. The building houses the human ego, conceived by the artistic imagination of humans and glorified to be a human-like god. The religious building is also a place to visit and ask the god for protection from the environment and from other humans.

The enclosed interior space of the building intended to contain and shelter the worshippers from the exterior natural environment, also has unintended meanings. The interior space represents an unseen, unmeasurable, and therefore irrational cosmological force of which the triune soul force is a continuation. This true insight is covered over for the human purpose of comprehension by utilizing the conception of a human-like god. The building encapsulates the conceived drug of a human-like god who will save those solemnly assembled from their own life sickness of an irrational triune soul force. The interior space also represents another dimension of reality, an afterlife that differs from the biological sensory reality consisting of dimensions of height, width, depth, and change of time.

Religion is art, defined as "works created by human skill and imagination." All religious buildings and relics, sculpted and painted images, and all written scriptures are works of art. A theistic religious building is for humans to consort in, and for a god to at least visit, if not set up housekeeping to dwell in. In reality a human-like god does not dwell in any building but only in the brains of the humans who assemble in the building. If a human-like god truly exists and wants to be revered and worshipped in a building on the earth, the god would and should surely build his own. Existing as a subjective conceived idea, this event will never occur. Instead the god is said to dwell distant from the earth, in a heaven. Is this heaven unlimited or a particular limited finite place located in infinity? It seems probable that only a local, limited god has an interest in humans while a nonlocal infinite entity would have unlimited infinite interests and its attention would range across infinite space and time and would not narrow to the finite limitation of humans.

Humans conceive and then believe that a human-like god exists. Humans then have to build temple dwellings for a human-like god, as it is quite evident that no god has ever built a dwelling on earth. If there exists no dwelling built by a god on earth, then it can be extrapolated there does not exist any dwelling place built by a god in another dimension. If a human-like god wants to instill trust and belief, then let him build his own grand temple dwelling place on earth for all to see. Then trust can increase and it can be accepted that the god has a dwelling place elsewhere. It is quite certain this will never happen as a human-like god is only an imaginary substitute for a truly poignant lack of human knowledge, kindness, respect, sensitivity, and love, and is only an imaginary model for the potential to develop these qualities in humans.

Death

A nonlocal cosmological force is ever existent, it exists prior to relative forces and to quantum energy particles that form the environment and life. From the ground of a cosmological force there is a continuous relative motion as a departing of quantum particles to form atoms and electrons that develop stars, planets, the earth, and life. From then on there is continual motion of the environment and movement of living forms. Like atoms and electrons, life must ever be in motion while awake and asleep until, the body ceases to move and enters the final rest of death.

The word death refers to the observation that a once living body dies and no longer moves, something has moved out of or away from it. Subconscious and conscious functions of willing and knowing are stored as memory in a physical brain and body. As a continuation of cosmological force, it is at least probable that memory may also be stored in a dimensional field and may continue after physical death separate from the body. While not empirically verified, the triune soul force and energy of the body once bound together may continue to display the phenomenon of coherence, defined as a quality or state of "sticking together, cohesion, a consistent relationship of parts." Supported by the laws of conservation of mass and energy, and quantum entanglement, physical death may be a transition and an awakening to another dimension of existence.

All that exists is conserved by a cosmological force. When destroyed by impact or time, material mass forms are conserved as smaller parting fragments of mass consisting of atoms and electrons. The physics theory of "quantum entanglement" also known as "quantum interconnectedness" also affect the conservation process. The theory is a tested scientific phenomenon in which independent quantum particles once interactive and then separate in space and time, display and preserve a connection with each other to form a quantum state or system regardless of space and time.

Therefore, the continual willing resistance of humans to have or not to have in life, may produce an energy and force pattern that after physical death is preserved.

Denouement

The human problem of identifying what brings all things into existence is solved by conceiving a human-like god. The famous or infamous declaration by the philosopher Friedrich Nietzsche (1844-1900) that "God is dead" is only half true. A human-like god has and will always be dead as an objective reality but does live in many a human brain as a subjective conceived idea. The concept of a human-like god is a focus of attention and a shortcut symbol to the origin of what exists; a place of safety in life and in death. A human-like god is not known to exist objectively but is known to exist for certain, only subjectively in the human brain. A god not sensed is a subjective and conceived nonsense god. The statement "god exists but is unknown" is to say it does not exist. Unknown cancels out the assertion of a god as objective to remain only subjective.

The question has long been asked, "Is there a god?" If the answer is that there is a human-like god who made the environment and life, oversees and variously causes or controls events, and waits after death to reward or punish, this is a false and wrong answer. If the answer is that a human-like god is an artistic model subjectively created by humans to explain where the environment and life came from, serves to imaginatively protect human life, and represents the potential of humans to achieve a higher level of knowing and doing, this is a true and right answer.

The majority of humans continue to be cognitively unable to trace the origin of life to the environment. Humans are also unable to detect a cosmological force that is immanent in the function of cells and organs of the body. The environment is non-conscious and does not readily respond to human needs. Humans do consciously respond to each other but mostly in subconscious antagonistic ways. Therefore, humans need some greater human-like conscious ability to respond and to control reality events of the environment and life. Humans are in dire need of better reasoning ability and in desperate need of a greater judging ability. The concept of a human-like god has been meticulously developed over many years, and even though imaginary, is accepted to be real by so many. Even though the idea of a human-like god is comforting, in reality it is only a subjective psychological response to the stress of living. It is no great wonder then, a cosmological force is architecturally plastered over with human attributes, to artistically form a human-like god so as to reinforce human efforts, while simultaneously diverting attention away from the reality of life experiences.

Life struggles to exist in the godless matrix and crucible of the environment, the shifting change of the elements that form the earth; the restless waters of the ocean, lakes, rivers, and rain, the air and wind, fluctuating temperature of heat and cold, light and dark. Life exists within narrow limits and boundaries that are continually changing. Life by necessity strains to adjust, and in so doing either under or over compensates and finds it difficult to properly balance. Balance is the "good" the only real and true "god" of life. All other gods are human-like fakes, artistic representations of the good of balance, a good only wrought by an individual who devotes time and cultivates the practice of self and soul exploration.

Being a member of a social group has the benefit of mutual support, but the cost is often "group think" and the atrophy of a richer depth of self and soul knowledge. Times spent in solitude and meditation remove attention from distracting sensations of outside objects, by focusing on inside sensations of breathing or parts of the body. Sensate picture images of outside objects slowly fade as a focus of attention increases to meditate on inside sensations of breathing or body. Distracting images of the outside fade like ethereal ghost images. With consistent meditation practice comes awareness of how attention to inside sensations is easily interrupted by picture images. Slowing conscious picture making of now moments, memory and imagination, subconscious content of forgotten memories and suppressed insights and knowledge surface in conscious awareness. There develops more clarity of intuition and psychic insight into situations of life.

Human consciousness is difficult to investigate as it separates into subject and object, and conscious and subconscious content. Consciousness is a continuation of the observed environment that is a continuation of an unobserved cosmological force. Both consciousness and a cosmological force cannot be directly observed. A human knower cannot know what consciousness is, only that it consists of structure and content. Consciousness cannot be directly observed. Only the phenomena of its contents, of brain willing and picture images, and body behaviors can be observed.

Meditation is a soteriological practice. Training attention increases conscious awareness of subconscious perception and memories, and develops sensitivity to subconscious body functions. Consistent practice of meditation contributes to reducing egocentrism and consequently to seeing situations more objectively. While meditation increases self and soul awareness while living, it also has soteriological value for post-death experience. Not meditatively increasing conscious self and soul awareness during life, after death the predominant subconscious habits of the triune soul force of hunger, sex, and aggression, may tend to repeat. To speculate, in keeping with the circular reality of atoms and electrons, solar systems and planets, rotating galaxies, and repetitive seasons and days and nights, the surviving soul might also repeat or reincarnate. These speculative musings do not fit well into the limited human time line and potential of humans as evidenced by Middle East and adopted by the Western religious myths. In the vast cosmic and quantum dimensions of space and time, human potential may be much more than previously considered.

The complex conscious human "self" has evolved from the subconscious "soul," from the non-conscious environment, and from a non-conscious cosmological force. As a continuation of a cosmological force, the soul of life is a singular force expressed in three ways, as hunger, sex, and reproduction, and aggression. Each triune force is distinct yet mutually supporting. Hunger for food supports sexual activity and aggression. Sex is often accompanied by aggression of partner dominance, control, and domestic violence. Conscious willing occurring in the brain for either food, sex, or aggression produces brain images that easily lead to behaviors to acquire the desired object. The conscious self of reasoning slaves for the subconscious will to live, the triune soul force.

Few humans appreciate the ability of their body to move. Life is wondrously and soundly rooted in the earth and solar environment that grows from a cosmological force. Consciousness is related to what and where life and the environment comes from, the non-phenomenon of a not observed cosmological force. A cosmological force cannot be observed. The relative reality of its contents of environment and living forms can be observed, investigated, and known. The traditional popular way to know an unknown cosmological force is accomplished by conceiving of and sharing a psychological overlay of a human-like god.

Artistic imagination has created a human-like god. Therefore, the last judgment after death by a human-like god can only be a conscious self-judgment of conscience and subconscious soul content in a multidimensional context. Any process of entering and exiting natural dimensions of reality is not directed by a human-like god but by the relative soul force of the individual. Humans falsely attribute a disembodied personality to an imagined human-like god and then in error conclude that if a human-like god can exist without a biological body, humans can also survive without a body in heaven. In reality, what is alluded to by this false view, is the true view that what moves within humans as a triune soul force is a continuation of a not destructible, non-human-like, and nonlocal cosmological force.

The essence of life is a metaphysical will to live. Without some kind of intentional effort and supporting environment, life cells composed of many intricate physical parts would not exist. The triune soul force of hunger, sex and reproduction, and aggression is a continuation of earth energy and a non-human cosmological force. Theistic religious tradition has projected the intentional effort to live, outside the individual life form and beyond the supportive environment of earth. The individual effort to live is intentionally misplaced and instead attributed to the whim and fiat of a human-like god. It is the soul of life that moves and saves an individual, not some puerile human species imagined first father god.

The soul is a relative continuation of an indestructible cosmological force, field, or ground. Based on the laws of conservation of energy, mass, and momentum, along with finer "entangled" energy elements of brain and body, some conscious and subconscious quality must remain after death. Life disappears from eyesight but as a continuation of energy, quantum particles, and cosmological force, by law its essence has to continue.